Get Your First Job as a Freelancer

10 Stories from Men in Freelancing

Arthur Lee

Arthur Lee Books
Melbourne, Australia

Copyright © 2021 Arthur Lee

www.arthurlee.com.au

All rights reserved. No part of this book may be reproduced, or stored in a retrieval system, or transmitted in any form or by any means, electronic, mechanical, photocopying, recording, or otherwise, without express written permission of the publisher.

Every effort has been made to trace or contact all copyright holders. The publishers will be pleased to make good any omissions or rectify any mistakes brought to their attention at the earliest opportunity.

ISBN: 9798467591780
Imprint: Independently published

Arthur Lee
PO Box 161, Forest Hill VIC 3131
Australia
ABN: 29 172 617 138

Contents

The pivot 1

Feed and grow your passion 5

A vision to help others through freelancing 11

Do your research, build a portfolio, complete your profile 17

Freelancing as an alternative to an 8 to 5 job 23

Getting your quotes right 31

Never start work without a contract 35

Be patient, polite and thankful 41

Freelancing as a university student 47

Trust yourself and work hard 53

Stay calm, don't think you are not going to make it . 59

Afterword 63

Acknowledgements

From top left to bottom right: A.H.M. Rashad Sorwar, Bryon Ngo, Diego Navarro, Ford Wanyonyi, Ishtiyaq Hussain, Lalit Khokhar, Muhammad Aulia Rahman, Pantelis Nikolopoulos, Seun Ajia, Thanadon Tantivit

The pivot

In my first book, I was writing my thoughts and thinking about some of the difficult times in business. Last time, I was at a cafe. Today's setting is a little bit different. It's 5am and still dark. I'm in my study. It's one of those days where I woke up in the middle of the night and found it impossible to go back to sleep. My mind was running wild with ideas.

I thought about a time in my earlier business life when I was stuck. It was about 12 years ago, and I couldn't find a way to take my business forward. It wasn't that I didn't do well. It's just that I couldn't wait around for things to happen by themselves either. Things were good, but rather than lying in bed awake for an hour, I decided to get up and start doing things instead.

The pathway I ended up taking was an interesting one. I picked a niche in my industry that was very poorly serviced and started to work on what the needs of my potential clients were. Then, I approached industry leaders to share my ideas. They all said that it couldn't be done, and I distinctly remember one person wishing me "good luck", but with a tone of sarcasm.

I gave it a try and hired an experienced person who had the skills to work in the area I had proposed. They agreed to help out with the main business while we worked together to develop the new service in the more niche area.

Late nights were spent on marketing letters to potential referrers. I applied the latest understanding of website building and SEO that I had learnt through online means, and most of all, I added my own flavor of creativity to the mix. It was a tough time, and it made me wonder if taking on this new area was the right choice.

I'll tell you a bit more about this journey in the final chapter, but for now I want to move along and introduce you to what you are about to read next.

In the following chapters, I asked men from different countries a few questions about their first job as a freelancer. Reading their responses was amazing because it took me back to those earlier times when I had to fight hard to get my first client, when I had to pivot to try and stand out from the crowd, and the feelings of despair. However, as I read of these men's successes, it also reminded me of my success in the early days.

These were the questions I asked.

Why did you want to become a freelancer? How did you get started?

How long did it take you to get your first job as a freelancer? Was it hard to get?

Was your experience in your first freelancing job a positive one?

What are your hopes as a freelancer? How far do you see your potential as a freelancer?

A word of wisdom for others wanting to get into freelancing work online.

I hope that you will be inspired by these stories. I hope that you can draw strength from the experience of these people. Maybe one day, you can share your story of success with those around you.

Get Your First Job as a Freelancer

Feed and grow your passion

Seun Ajia - Nigeria

Why did you want to become a freelancer? How did you get started?

Freelancing was not an option when I was younger. Growing up, I didn't have any goals or dreams, and went with life's flow. Unfortunately, or better put, fortunately, life threw me out of my comfort zone. Being out of my comfort zone made me question life and its meaning; why do I exist, and what is my purpose?

In the quest to answer these questions, I fell into depression and had suicidal tendencies. It felt like the more questions I asked, the more I struggled for answers. I had to do something fast because I was losing my mind. I needed some time alone, so I resigned from my work as an accountant and moved back into my parent's house.

For a while, I lived on the money I had saved whilst I had been working. It was also around this time that I was introduced to making money online.

I started with affiliate marketing, moved onto motivational writing and finally, took up storytelling. Throughout this process, I was finding and piecing myself back together. Whilst I was awful at writing during my school years, it had now become therapeutic and my way of connecting to the world. In June of 2021, I stopped writing for likes, comments, and praise, and turned it into a business instead.

I dedicated myself to freelancing and specifically, to the writing niche.

Freelancing has not only become a source of income, but a way for me to express myself to my family, friends, and the world at large.

Always try to find the "Why" of your freelance journey. No doubt it will be money-related, but you must find the deeper essence behind the need for it too. When found, this answer will give you the strength to push on during tough times.

How long did it take you to get your first client? Was it hard to get?

I'm a perfectionist, so when I picked up writing, I noticed I wasn't good enough to produce quality articles, stories, or pieces for others. So, I learned. For two years, I signed up to competitions from which I received feedback I dedicated myself to reading books and multiple articles per day. I also went back to the basics of grammar and punctuation and made friends online who helped me on my journey.

I signed up to an online marketplace that brings freelancers and clients together. Before signing up, I read a ton of articles online and subscribed to other freelancers telling their stories. Reading these articles and stories gave me confidence. It also gave me a sneak peek as to what I could expect from the platform.

Because I had accumulated experience while learning the art of writing, and had gathered information on the marketplace platform, getting my first client wasn't problematic. I was hired for my first job in the same week that I had registered on the platform. It was a low-paying job, but it helped me to launch my services.

The client was so impressed that she left a beautiful review and tried to engage me on longer term basis., I ended up declining because the pay was low. Just days later, I ended up getting a job that paid 20 times better.

Devote yourself to your first job. At first, try to do one job at a time to gain trust and deliver quality work. Human beings tend to stick with what they are familiar with, instead of trying out new things. This rule also applies to freelancers. Clients prefer to stick with a competent and trustworthy freelancer with whom they've had past engagements, rather than taking the risk of trying out a new one. Make sure you hold on to clients for repeat business, as that's how you will grow your business.

Was your experience in your first freelancing job a positive one? Or a negative?

My first experience was a mixed one. The client's job title was "5 dollars for a 3000-word article". It wasn't the most appealing offer, but I bid for it and got the job. My impression was that I would just be writing a single 3000-word article for 5 dollars. After submitting the 3000 word piece, the client informed me that it was three 1000-word articles, and not a single 3000-word piece.

I was furious because I felt the client played me for a fool. I mean, who in their right mind would write three separate articles for 5 dollars. Just in case you're not in the writing niche and may not understand, writing requires you to carry out research, type your words, edit those words, and then submit them for review. I would have to complete this process three times instead of once, and she had purposely not communicated this crucial information to me.

Since I was already in, I gave my best and fought for an excellent review. The experience wasn't the most pleasant, but I moved on and made sure the quality of my work spoke for itself. After the contract, I tried negotiating the payment terms to a better one, but the client refused to improve it, and we went our separate ways.

Learn to be patient with clients. My first two clients had communication issues, but patience helped me to keep my relationship with them.

What are your hopes as a freelancer? How far do you see your potential as a freelancer?

My hope is that freelancing will continue to open doors for me to meet new people, secure more opportunities, and of course, earn more money.

One of my aims of becoming a freelancer was freedom and freelancing certainly gave me wings. Not only physically, but mentally too. I can't perform if I can't connect with an organization's vision or if its structure is rigid. I question why I studied Accounting and Finance, since such a course would land me in such rigid environments.

Thankfully, freelancing has saved me and given me a dream. I also aim to grow as a freelancer on the platform and slowly introduce myself to other social media platforms. The aim is to start an agency where we collect writing projects and deliver quality service to our clients.

As for my potential, I do not see a ceiling or a limit on how much I can grow. I am open to different writing styles but favor creative writing. There is much more to learn, and so I look forward to learning something new every day.

If freelancing is a part-time job for you, you should be more expressive and less tense when dealing with clients. Create an environment that you can thrive in and not one that will choke you.

A word of wisdom for others wanting to get into freelancing work online

One thing I have noticed is that some freelancers lack patience. In this line of work, patience is an important virtue to have, be it in relation to your self-development, the amount you charge when you start your journey, or the dedicated hours you put into the work. Like every business, the freelancer business is a sole proprietorship, meaning that you have to run it like a true business, which of course, includes giving it time to grow.

Strategies and techniques that work well for other people may not work for you. What makes freelancing unique is that no two cases are the same. Understanding yourself, your personality and your goals will go a long way in determining how you operate your business. A part of freelancing is allowing your individuality to shine, and this will become one of your defining features as you grow.

Additionally, learn to track the income and expenses of your freelance business. Reinvest some of that profit back into the business or other investment options to avoid using all your profit (if you can afford to do so).

My last point is always to remember that the customer is king. Try as much as possible to fulfill the requirements of your client. Remember, this doesn't mean you should always follow instructions, especially not if those instructions go against your core principles as an individual. The blend of a strong character and ability to provide an excellent service will take you far.

A vision to help others through freelancing

A.H.M. Rashad Sorwar - Bangladesh

Why did you want to become a freelancer? How did you get started?

Greenery all around, the chirping of birds, the sweet light and heat of the morning sun, a pond in front, a crop field on the horizon in front of it, with a small reading table in the middle, a small sitting chair, a cup of coffee and a laptop. Far from the concrete and robotic city, I serve clients on all continents through freelancing.

My closest friend has an MBA from the best university in Bangladesh with a degree in Telecommunications. He is one of the top-rated freelancers in the world today and I came to this path mainly through being inspired by him.

I have an MBA in Marketing and BS degree in Computer Science and Engineering. Whilst I started as a technical person, I later diverted my professional life to the business sector. I have had five jobs in the fourteen years of my career.

I asked myself which profession would also allow me to give my family time, live independently with nature and derive a source of income. I don't think that there exists a better option in the world than freelancing.

On the same day that I realized this, I registered onto a freelancing site and started submitting proposals.

How long did it take you to get your first client? Was it hard to get?

Despite opening an account on a freelancing site 2 years ago today, I didn't use it. However, in the last two weeks, I updated my profile causing the platform to accept it and publish it as a verified profile. This is where I started. On the first day, I submitted about 17 proposals, two of which resulted in interview calls. One person asked me questions and didn't end up going ahead with my profile, but another person from the Netherlands put their trust in me and let me write an article.

It took me a day to get this first job. I chose only to show the jobs I love as a skill on my profile, which could be why my client trusted me. When I delivered on the first job, the customer was happy and gave me a five-star review.

Being able to deliver the first job successfully gave me a lot of confidence. I want to use it in later life, just like in preparation for retirement. We have a proverb in Bangladesh that "hobby has no weight". Since writing is a passion, I think that people will find me if I stick with it. After getting my first job, I was hired for a total of four jobs in one week.

Was your experience in your first freelancing job a positive one?

Of course, it was positive. I finished my first job with great enthusiasm. The job had been a brand new experience. Being a citizen of a Muslim country, I had zero knowledge about casinos. They were something that I had never seen or known about.

In order to write about them, I had to do a lot of reading and research. This profession helps me to understand subjects that I previously had no knowledge of. I was hired for a job that I had never done in my life, I had to deliver it for the satisfaction of the client, and I also had the opportunity to develop myself. This is the advantage of this profession. You are constantly learning new things and establishing yourself as a dynamic person. I don't know whether there is a bigger positive than this in the world.

All of the legendary people in this world have been through changes. They were broken into pieces and put themselves back together. That's how they grew. I want to grow in the same way. As I said before, I was a technical person before I came to the business sector. I considered myself successful whilst on both of these paths, just as I want to be successful here.

What are your hopes as a freelancer? How far do you see your potential as a freelancer?

As I said before, I want to move far away from the city. We, as citizens of the third world, once had problems with connectivity. At present, our country no longer has this problem.

I want to make an organic farm. On my farm, I'll produce crops and vegetables, fish will be farmed, and there will be livestock and poultry. All the while, my freelancing will continue. I don't think there is a better profession in the world than one that allows you to live amongst nature.

My spouse is a doctor, and she also wants to go back to the village to provide medical care to the poor and needy.

To achieve these things, I'll need the help of other people. To hire these people, I'll have to be top-rated freelancer; a status that I wish to achieve in the next 6 to 12 months.

There is nothing in the world that people cannot do. My thoughts are very small compared to others. Today, people want to settle on Mars today and people like Jeff Bezos and Richard Branson are orbiting space. There's a quotation, "To the whole world you are the someone, and to the someone, you are the whole world." The people that I end up employing, I want to be the whole world, and not just someone to them.

A word of wisdom for others wanting to get into freelancing work online.

I want to be a freelancer for a noble cause. I want to live with nature and my family, build organic farms, give jobs to people, and improve human resources. At least one hundred and eighty million people live in Bangladesh. The people of our country are now becoming educated, and the literacy rate is 72.76 percent. If I could create jobs for some people of this huge population, I would consider myself blessed.

If I can make the decision to freelance after working for almost a decade, then those who are young and still have a lot of time on their hands can too. There is nothing better in this world than spending time with family.

Traditional jobs are not everything, and you don't want to make yourself mentally ill. Many people become emotionally upset while enduring the tension that comes with traditional jobs, especially in this part of the world. Moreover, this pandemic has shaken people not only in our country but all over the world; billions of people have lost their traditional jobs. However, the scope of work for freelancers has increased.

The biggest advantage of freelancing is that I can do exactly what I love to do. If you want a traditional job, you must work hard outside of your passion, which may not be ideal. Many people in Bangladesh are not very educated, but they have become self-sufficient by freelancing.

It's never too late to find your skills, work, arrange employment, love people, and let people love you too.

Get Your First Job as a Freelancer

Do your research, build a portfolio, complete your profile

Muhammad Aulia Rahman - Indonesia

Why did you want to become a freelancer? How did you get started?

I decided to become a freelancer because of the pandemic situation in my country. Lockdown conditions and restrictions on office activities that occur here in my country have restricted my activities both in and out of the office. The restrictions placed on activities have forced me to work from home and evoked my old habits of writing, reading, and producing music.

Since this point, I had been looking for work online as a freelancer to write poetry, short stories, and song lyrics.

In addition, being a freelancer allows you to manage your time more freely. I think that this is good for the mind because freelancers are less likely to suffer from the burnout effects of routine office work.

I've done freelancing jobs many times and I got these jobs because of the information conveyed in my circle of friends. However, the jobs I could take were limited due to unclear job availability, difficulty in payment processing, and perhaps even worse, fraud.

During the pandemic, I also had plenty of free time available to meet new people virtually or online. That's when I discovered freelance job sites.

How long did it take you to get your first client? Was it hard to get?

I got my first two clients within sixteen days. Getting hired for jobs on these freelancing websites is quite tricky because they're very competitive and professional platforms. In the writing category, it seems that there are many experienced freelancers with thick portfolios.

When it came to statistics, in the first month I applied for 33 jobs related to writing, at both entry and intermediate level. Only two of these jobs were accepted. In the first week, I made a fatal mistake. I copy and pasted cover letters to apply to various job vacancies, and many of my proposals were declined.

Due to frequent rejections, I decided to read the forums, communities, and help and support. That's where I learned tips and tricks on how to get your proposal considered. I had to have a personal yet professional cover letter. I had to find out what prospective clients wanted by reading their job descriptions and writing my cover letters based on these.

Meanwhile, in my other area of expertise, music (including song writing, mixing, and mastering), the number of jobs was very limited. I found it hard to compete in the field of audio expertise because my skills in the area are mediocre. In the future, I may leave the field of music and instead, focus solely on improving my writing method and honing my English skills.

Was your experience in your first freelancing job a positive one? Or a negative?

Since I was hired for my first two jobs at the same time, I'll tell you about both. For one of these projects, I found the experience to be positive, but it seems that my client wouldn't agree. This made me uncomfortable and afraid that the work that I had completed was incorrect and worthless.

My first job was for a research project. In the job description, this job has 5 stages/milestones. Payments were made at each stage or milestone. After the contract was offered, I received and filled out the research questionnaire form. I took it seriously and felt I that I had done my best.

Then, I notified the client that I had filled out the form and asked what I should do next. The client said, "Please be patient. The project will start in a few days. We will inform you." Two days later, the client paid me for the first milestone, but then he terminated the contract!

As a newbie who was very excited to complete my first job, I felt really bad. I tried to work out if I had made errors when filling out the form, grammar errors perhaps. To this day, I still don't know what went wrong, and haven't dared to ask why the contract was terminated.

The other contract was for a project writing blog articles about business and the life of expatriates. This time, my client was an expert in writing blog articles; this was evident from the clear instructions, guidelines, and given format. The comments and revisions provided were also very technical. In general, this contract went quite well.

What are your hopes as a freelancer? How far do you see your potential as a freelancer?

To be honest, at first, I didn't expect anything. However, as I continue to apply for more jobs and work on ongoing projects, both online and offline, I wish that I could quit my regular job and freelance forever. It's not that I'm not grateful, but just imagine, I've spent years working on annual reports, financial reports in the office, and managing and compiling a contract agreement with contents that vary little from year to year.

Ultimately, I feel that this will probably make me lose my passion and ideals. Maybe these are very clichéd words, but if being a freelancer makes you happy, being a writer makes you think, and being a musician makes you feel valuable, then it sounds like a profession worth pursuing.

I realize that my potential can still be developed and is far from complete. As the saying goes, my journey and potential is still far, as far as the eye can see (unfortunately I have myopia). I feel that as a freelancer, there is no limit in choosing skills and developing thoughts. All things can be learned, and all things can be done. The sky's the limit!

Everything is interconnected. What you did yesterday affects what you do today. If you didn't do anything yesterday, you and I wouldn't be here today. Now, I can work on optimizing the skills that I already have. In doing so, I'm sure I will learn more and discover new skills.

A word of wisdom for others wanting to get into freelancing work online.

Just do it. Do it and you will fall in love with it. But of course, it requires special preparation to be able to compete on a very open, fair, and professional freelancing platform.

Here are some points that I think are important:

Do a little research. There are many articles and blogs on the internet. Pay attention and do a little research about what freelance job market is the best for you to enter. Decide on which skills you plan on offering to the world.

Build a portfolio. Hone your skills in your chosen field. Believe that above the sky, there is more sky. Perhaps you are the student with the greatest ability at your university. As a freelancer, success depends on your portfolio, badges, language skills, and other statistics. Don't be afraid to take on an easy entry level experience job as it will be useful to add to your portfolio and hone your skills. Be patient and allow time for your statistics to grow. In turn, your profile will become fuller, and you'll be able to attract more clients.

Your profile is your exhibition. Complete your online profile. Showcase your proud experiences and certificates of expertise. Complete skill tests. When submitting a proposal, consider the level of experience, education, and length of time required for the completion of the contract as stated by the client in the job description.

Good luck to my friends out there who want to start a career as a freelancer.

Freelancing as an alternative to an 8 to 5 job

Ford Wanyonyi - Kenya

Why did you want to become a freelancer? How did you get started?

Working online is easy, flexible, and lucrative. However, it comes with its fair share of challenges. Typically, choosing to be a freelancer requires careful consideration of many factors.

I became a freelancer for three main reasons.

First, I wanted to earn extra income. Yes, I had an 8 to5 job, but I was unable to meet all of my needs. So, I took up freelancing to help meet my expenses and increase my savings.

Second, I liked the flexibility that came with freelancing. I can schedule when I work, for instance, to work at times when I'm most creative and productive. This type of freedom, convenience, and flexibility is what I admire most.

Lastly, I lost my 8 to 5 job so I had no other source of income other than freelancing. That pushed me to become a full-time freelancer to ensure that I was able to earn a living. Freelancing became my best alternative, and since I was familiar with the freelancing scene, manoeuvring was easy.

When I started as a freelancer, it wasn't forthcoming. I didn't get a job at first. Then, one day, a friend told me about an online freelancing website, and since I wanted extra cash, I thought I should give it a try. I created an account and ensured that my profile was 100% completed. The profile serves as a resume and is the key to getting hired. So, I had to curate it to attract clients in the niche in which I was seeking work.

A complete profile has a title and overview, photo, education background, language proficiency, contact details, hourly rate, and past work experience. I had created a standout profile. The real task was yet to come - creating winning proposals.

How long did it take you to get your first client? Was it hard to get?

I landed my first job as an online freelancer after three weeks, but I could have landed it earlier if I had known a few things. My biggest mistake was applying for any and every job posted, without knowing what it really entailed. I applied for four positions in seven days!

For two weeks, I only received one job interview. It was from a client with an unverified payment method, and I had been warned against such clients. Towards the end of the second week, I read about being more aggressive when applying for jobs, i.e., applying for as many as possible. Also, I realized that since I was just getting started, I should apply for entry-level positions.

I took this advice seriously, and for the next three days, I applied for 30 jobs, each of which cost me two connection credits (we get 60 free credits each month). According to a friend, the best time to apply for jobs was after the 15th of the month because by this point, most other freelancers would have exhausted their credits and I would have a better chance.

I don't know which of my new methods worked, but I ended up getting six interviews! It was amazing. Out of the six interviews, I landed three gigs. They paid close to nothing.

Really, how could you consider $1 for writing 1000 words? I accepted these jobs because I wanted a good rating on my online profile. Fortunately, they were short-term contracts, and all of the clients gave me a magnificent 5-star rating. I gave all of the projects my best; all of my thoughts and efforts.

Whilst completing these meagre-paying jobs, I continued searching for better-paying jobs.

Was your experience in your first freelancing job a positive one?

Positive! My first freelancing job ran for two weeks after which the client informed me that he had no more work. He ended the contract and gave me a five-star rating. His words were "fast, dependable, thanks!" Though the pay was small, this feedback gave me the motivation to work harder and smarter.

The jobs were not that easy. They were long articles on topics that there was very little information available on (or maybe I didn't know how to use search engines). Besides, they were SEO articles, and I didn't have much experience with keyword usage. But I didn't let this opportunity pass by. It was time to learn and to please the client.

I aimed to make this client a repeat client. I remember going over various web pages and searching for SEO writing skills and techniques. I made notes on various aspects of freelancing, including how to get better-paying clients.

Freelancing is a type of dance, a dance that I must lead. The primary rule is that the client comes first. Thus, doing the best job to help the client get what they want is vital. The in-depth research will also help me to get what I want – good money and polished skills.

Later, the client came back to me, but this time with better rates. The most challenging thing as a new freelancer is knowing how much to charge. In most cases, clients set the amount, and this could leave you in a vulnerable spot.

What are your hopes as a freelancer? How far do you see your potential as a freelancer?

One thing is clear: if I do a great job, I'll be asked to do more.

Though my primary goal of being a freelancer was not to be a writer, I've found myself being one. I have changed roles over time from a mere content creator, to managing a team of writers, to virtual assistance. Each task I've laid my hands on, I've completed from my heart. This way, as well as making my clients happy, I am able to learn and better myself.

Currently, I'm a full-time freelancer, and I intend on things staying this way. Through freelancing, I've been able to create multiple cash flow streams whilst leaving clients happy. Beyond money, I've deeply integrated myself into the freelancing system, and I can see the benefits of freelancing that people speak about. For instance, I can choose the clients I want, control my workload, work on varied projects with great exposure, and retain much-needed flexibility and independence. Indeed, this is impressive to me.

Since the gig economy is fast expanding, I want to stay part of it for as long as it survives. For the past three and a half years, I've grown my potential as a writer. Though I began as a web content creator, changing roles has exposed me to different types of writing.

My first income was $75 a month – it was meagre. However, after two months, I started seeing my best days, when my average monthly income was over $400. Today, I still strive to earn more each month. Currently, I am targeting at least $800 a month.

A word of wisdom for others wanting to get into freelancing work online

Getting into freelancing can be exciting. For most people, it's all about making money. Yes, there is money, but it isn't easy money. Before you get started, ensure you have the following:

A complete profile. Clients will want to know your credentials and freelancing experience. While creating your profile, the information must be 100% accurate – honesty is critical. Clearly define the tasks that you can handle.

Avoid unnecessary pressure. It isn't a sprint, it's a marathon. Online freelancing sites have jobs for every freelancer. Approach the platforms with a clear mind and only select jobs that are compatible with your profile. You can make these sites revolve around you!

There is a lot of learning entailed. Apart from polishing your skills, you'll need to learn new skills to remain relevant. Remember, new software is generated daily to aid freelancers, so you'll need to upskill to remain relevant.

Be patient. Things may not bloom in your first week, or even in your first month. Don't give up. Continue writing proposals whilst polishing your talents and skills. Soon, you'll land your dream job.

Start freelancing as a side hustle. Simply put, be sure to have another source of income while you're setting up your freelancing career.

Be committed. Always approach or respond to clients wisely. Some clients may offer you jobs but be demeaning and rude. Such unexpected responses should not deter you from your set goals. Brush it off wisely and make relevant changes.

Follow the client's instructions thoroughly, and when something isn't clear, seek clarification. The job belongs to the client unless they ask you to be creative with it.

Freelancing is a cycle of "feast or famine." Sometimes, you'll have plenty of work that you may be unable to handle by yourself. Other times, you may not have even a single job, even from the lowest paying client. So, permanently save for the famine period.

Keep the network alive. Tell everyone from your oldest client to local businesses that you're a freelancer. If possible, set up a website. You can also use social networks to get clients. The point is to make sure that you're always prospecting. If you are a copywriter, connect with other copywriters in your field. They may well refer you when the need arises. Be sure not to keep your eggs in one basket.

Get Your First Job as a Freelancer

Getting your quotes right

Lalit Khokhar - India

Why did you want to become a freelancer? How did you get started?

Let me tell you something about my regular job. For the past three years, I have been working n a government office as a Junior Assistant in Delhi. It's a clerical job with a salary of around 29,000 INR. I am also a tech enthusiast and find it fascinating to learn about computer software and hardware.

I had several reasons for wanting to become a freelancer. First, I had free time due to a nationwide lockdown in my country in April of 2021. I was sitting idle at home and wanted to utilize my free time to do something productive. My mind is always thinking of ways to increase my disposable income.

I was always drawn to freelancer jobs but previously, I didn't have the resources or time. I started searching for freelancer websites and became aware of two popular ones. I registered myself on both but I preferred the one that allowed me to apply for listed jobs.

I started with admin assistant skills as in my regular job, I complete data entry and organization. Later on, I discovered the other services that I could offer such as PDF editing, form creation, photo editing, etc. I read the help articles on how to set up my profile in the best way for my potential clients and proceeded to set my profile up.

How long did it take you to get your first client? Was it hard to get?

It took around 15-20 days to secure my first client. I was desperately trying to get an answer to my proposals, but even after applying for more than 15 jobs, I didn't receive any responses. I ran out of connection credits that were required to submit proposals. I became somewhat irritated that even though I wrote good proposals and had the skills required for jobs I was applying for, I still hadn't gained my first client.

I wanted to apply for more jobs, so I bought a premium plan and started applying again. I applied with the lowest possible fee for each job. I tried to improve my proposal writing by researching best practices for proposal writing and learned new skills relating to common jobs.

Finally, on May 4th, 2021, I got my first client. They were looking for a freelancer to create a fillable PDF form. I was so happy to receive a reply and agreed to whatever price was offered by the client.

Was your experience in your first freelancing job a positive one?

I would say it was a positive one. I may have not earned enough for the time invested, but I was happy that I got my first client, and I had a feeling that it would be better from here on. I would finally have a rating on my profile, which I believed would compel other clients to offer me projects.

I spent a whole day completing my first job just for $5, but I was happy and did my best to deliver the best possible results because it was for my very first client. Thankfully, the client was very cooperative and answered all of my queries patiently.

What are your hopes as a freelancer? How far do you see your potential as a freelancer?

As a freelancer, I want to be valued as a skilled person so that I can land clients who are looking for good quality work. I am regularly learning new skills to improve my knowledge and capabilities so I can get to work with more clients and different types of projects. Currently, I am learning web development.

I hope to increase my potential earnings from freelancer jobs, and someday, I hope to become a full-time freelancer and leave my regular job to work from home.

I am positive about my potential as a freelancer and as I grow my skill base and expertise, I can really see myself growing in this freelancing world. I see myself as a full-time freelancer with skills that are sought after by many.

A word of wisdom for others wanting to get into freelancing work online

Improve your skills and become an expert in any one field. Focus on your presentation and writing good proposals, and always be true to yourself and your client. Only apply for the jobs that are within your domain of skills. Keep learning and have patience.

I was very impatient when I started and was applying for all kinds of jobs without evaluating how much time it would take to complete the job, and what price I was quoting for it. On my second job, I applied for a job for $8 but when I sat down to complete the job, I realized that it would take 3 days to complete, which was far beyond my expectation.

I asked the client to revise the contract amount and was lucky to have a generous client who increased the contract amount to $50. Unfortunately, not all clients are this generous, so be sure to always evaluate the job requirements and only apply if you can deliver the desired results within the specified budget and timeframe.

Quoting less is okay in your initial stages as a freelancer, but your earnings should be worth the time spent, at the very least. In fact, many clients avoid freelancers with low prices because they assume that the freelancer may not have the skillset that they're looking for.

Never start work without a contract

Pantelis Nikolopoulos - Greece

Why did you want to become a freelancer? How did you get started?

I've always been a fan of traveling the world and living a "free life", but I also understand that in order to do that, I have to be making some money. That's when I started looking for careers that fit my ambitions, and soon enough, I found freelance writing. It included copywriting and content writing, and I loved it. It's exactly what I wanted, so I began working on developing my skills.

I educated myself in the craft of copywriting for a year. I watched videos, took courses, read, and did everything that was necessary to succeed.

When I felt ready, I signed up for freelancing sites. I created my website and started growing my network. I created social media profiles and essentially made myself available for anyone that wanted to work with me!

Next, I had to mentally prepare myself for what was coming. I was a shy person so the thought of joining a Zoom call with a stranger was frightening. It took me a lot of time to get used to the idea, but I finally became comfortable with it.

Since I was both practically and mentally prepared, my freelance copywriting career had begun!

How long did it take you to get your first job as a freelancer? Was it hard to get?

I knew that I had zero experience so that if I wanted to land a job, I had to be qualitative and provide massive value, and that's what I did. I applied for jobs that I was truly interested in, rather than random ones. I read each job post very carefully and tried to understand every aspect of it.

I offered very low rates because it was the only way to land a job. My cover letters were written very carefully too. I had to communicate who I was, what I do, why I do it, and why I was perfect for the job. It wasn't easy. My first proposals never received responses, but that was the norm for every new freelancer out there.

After applying for many jobs, I finally got a response. It was from a site that was buying and selling random things, but I didn't really care about the quality of the site. I was just excited and thrilled that I had my first job. It was a start, and I was very proud of myself.

Was your experience in your first freelancing job a positive one?

Unfortunately, my first job ended up being a negative experience. Here's what happened. I was supposed to proofread a page of a website and correct any mistakes that it had. Then, I had to take the correct content and add it to the HTML of the website. All of that for $10 ($8 after Upwork fees). The client told me to start working on it. I asked for the contract, but he told me that we would sign it once the job was completed. I didn't give it another thought and started the work.

After I had corrected and added the content to the website, the client told me that there was a little more content to correct and add, but it wasn't ready yet. We agreed to continue the next day. When the next day came, he told me that I would have to correct 50-100 articles, add them to the website, and create more pages. All that for $8! I couldn't accept that offer so I ended the conversation. He took the free content and left.

I was positive that he would give me the money, but he hadn't been clear on the terms. If I had known that from the start, I never would have accepted the project. Moral of the story? Never work without a contract; you're basically giving away your time for free.

What are your hopes as a freelancer? How far do you see your potential as a freelancer?

When I think of freelancing, one word comes to my mind - "career". It's my career and what I want to do with my life. It's my dream job and I don't plan on changing it. The university that I will attend will also be related to what I do.

10 years from now, I can see myself as the CEO of a big marketing or writing company. I'll have so much experience that I'll be forced to reject job proposals because I won't have the time to complete them. I will be fulfilled and proud of my life. Because of my

job, I'll be able to travel the world and make my dreams come true. I will teach other people how amazing it is to have a job that you love. I will constantly grow my company, and myself.

But before I make all of that happen, I have to lay the foundation. For me, freelancing sites are the way to do that; finding clients, building long-term relationships, and providing value to help businesses grow.

A word of wisdom for others wanting to get into freelancing work online

Do you love freelancing? Do you want to make it your full career? Is it your dream job? Then go for it! Go for it and never give up! You might fail 1, 2, 3, or 27 times but you only need to succeed once. That's it, just once.

Be wise about how you spend your time. Don't scroll non-stop through social media, play video games, and watch television all day. Every minute that you're not working, you should spend learning. That's the only way to reach the top.

Start small and work your way to the top. It will be hard, and it will certainly take time and a lot of effort, but it will be 100% worth it.

One last thing, never start working without a contract, especially on freelancing sites. You might not get paid, or you might end up doing something different than you imagined. It always becomes tricky, so try to avoid it. Be qualitative, always give value, and don't try to make it happen quickly. Beauty is in the process, always remember that!

Get Your First Job as a Freelancer

Be patient, polite and thankful

Bryan Ngo - Malaysia

Why did you want to become a freelancer? How did you get started?

To be completely honest, becoming a freelancer had never crossed my mind. If you had told me three years ago that one day, I would be an online freelance writer, I would have been very surprised. Back then, I had never heard of the word "freelancer", let alone thought of it as a job.

Since I was younger, my goal had always been to be a doctor, and I had never considered any other job as an option. After my high school graduation while I was waiting for my university admission, the Covid-19 pandemic had hit our country hard. So, I resolved to search for jobs online to support my family, as the pandemic meant that we were all suffering financially.

Both of my parents had lost their jobs and as the eldest child, I had no choice but to think of a way out and to help my family. I started researching online and, looking for jobs that would allow me to work from home as the lockdown restricted people from setting foot outside their house, even for work. I stumbled upon an article about how fresh graduates can earn money online, and I was hooked!

I resolved to do more research, and after a few articles and videos, voila! I came across one of the largest freelancing platforms which allowed anyone to kick-start their freelancing career. From there onwards, my course to become a professional freelance writer began.

How long did it take you to get your first client? Was it hard to get?

I would be lying if I told you that getting my first client was a piece of cake. It wasn't, and in fact, it was far from easy. I consider myself blessed in getting my very first client. I hadn't sent him a proposal. Rather, he was the one who found me.

Allow me to share my story...

I first created my online freelancer account on the 16th of July. It was my very first time on a platform like this, and I had no idea how it worked. I remember blindly sending proposals, and therefore using almost all my available connection credits. A new account provides you 50 credits, and I remember spending 42 of them on the first and second day, copying and pasting all of my proposals and sending them to all of the jobs that interested me.

I recall waking up on the third day and eagerly checking my phone to see if I had received any offers for any job postings. To my bewilderment, I hadn't received anything! Curious, and beginning to think that it was a scam, I decided to do some more research, liaise with the online community, and look through more videos on landing jobs. To my surprise, landing a job wasn't as easy as it first seemed. I discovered that to land a job, one had to send a great proposal, have a solid profile, and most importantly, many clients would prefer to hire someone with experience in the field.

Therefore, I immediately redesigned my profile. I highlighted my skills and created a specialized profile that made it easier for clients to search for and hire me for their job. Next, I sent a few well-written proposals and hoped for a better result in the next few days. To my dismay, there were no clients that accepted my proposals. I felt extremely disappointed and was ready to give up when I saw a red dot appear over my inbox, indicating that I had a message from a client.

Curious, I opened the message. It was from a client seeking freelancers for his job. He had found my profile and was content with it, so he sent an offer. I remember being so glad that before going into the interview with him and agreeing to take up the job, I had to compose my reaction.

Was your experience in your first freelancing job a positive one?

Let me assure you, it was 100% a positive one. I can't help but think back to the day when I accepted his offer. The job scope was to write a script for an online video as well as to provide the script's content.

I had lots of experience completing creative and descriptive writing so it wasn't a complex job for me. However, because it was my first job, I remember asking him tons of questions because I didn't want to mess anything up. I was sure to obtain clarity on all of his requirements, including the fonts and the written content format. I wanted to make sure that everything was perfectly fine for him.

He gave me a deadline of 6 days for the job. I was so enthusiastic that I completed the job that very same day. I worked until 2am and triple-checked the work before submitting it to him. What surprised me was his concern towards me. He asked me to not work until such late hours, and to remember to put my health first, especially given the pandemic. Man, I was touched! We always think of our clients as our boss, so much so that we may develop fear or uneasiness when we talk to them. But actually, they are human beings just like us.

I remember asking him to leave a review for me so that I could establish my online freelance profile. He did, and his words towards me were surprisingly kind and encouraging. *"This freelancer was such a joy to work with. He provided me with such a great service and I more than recommend his services."* To *my first client,* I will always remember you.

What are your hopes as a freelancer? How far do you see your potential as a freelancer?

I used to think that freelancing was not a good fit for me. If you had asked me this question a few years ago, I wouldn't have an answer. But now that I've given it a shot, I have to tell you that the perks of freelancing are surprisingly great.

First of all, when you work as a freelancer, you are your own boss. You're 100% in charge of your own freelance business. There is no need to worry about any schedule, no need to worry about the work location, and no need to worry about not being able to do the things that you love. "Do what you love, and you will never work another day in your life". This is one of my favorite quotes, and one that I always like to share with my readers.

How far do I see my potential as a freelancer? Well, let me assure you of this -as long as I can still read and write, I will always be a freelance writer, whether part-time or full-time. I've always enjoyed reading and writing novels, and my published works have been read by hundreds, if not thousands of readers. I bring joy by creating worlds with words and turning thoughts into words. It's a hobby that I will never stop doing.

A word of wisdom for others wanting to get into freelancing work online

I would like to share my thoughts on the three stages of being a freelancer. Bear in mind that this is just my humble opinion for those who are keen to get into the freelancing world.

Be patient. I know how hard it is to not land a job despite having a good profile and sending tons of good proposals, just because you don't have any experience. I understand how frustrating it is, but there are actually a few ways that you can try to land your first job. First, attempt to apply for smaller jobs first, complete them successfully, and receive good reviews from your clients. These will help you to establish a better and more professional profile that attracts clients when they read your cover letter.

Be polite to your clients! When you finally receive your first job, make sure to complete everything according to your client's request. Ask him or her questions and communicate more with them. You never know, they might see the potential in you and decide to hire you for their next job!

Be Thankful. Be thankful that you managed to land your first job. Be thankful when your clients leave you good reviews. Most importantly of all, be thankful that you have been given a chance to learn something new and gain experience, while being able to do what you enjoy the most. It's a dream come true.

Freelancing as a university student

Thanadon Tantivit - Thailand

Why did you want to become a freelancer? How did you get started?

The reasons I wanted to become a freelancer were rather spontaneous due to the Covid-19 pandemic. I wanted to do something during the summer holidays. I am a university student and over the past months, my plans have been turned upside down. Work in Phuket, Thailand, which heavily relies on tourism, has dried up. Also, travel to other parts of the country has been restricted, and in some cases, completely banned. This made any chance of finding a job, or activity to do, almost zero.

As such, I decided to become a freelance copywriter and content writer in order to kill time due to my experiences writing multiple reports, while at the same time, making a small amount of income to use later when I'm back at university. I was surprised to find out that my university classmates were freelance writers too. They were tremendously helpful in giving me advice on where to start and the types of job I should strive to start with. I would say that freelancing was a great way to use my passions to make money.

How long did it take you to get your first client? Was it hard to get?

It took me about two weeks before I got a reply from any of the employers. After submitting to over half a dozen job openings, competition from more experienced freelancers means that the clients may not choose you, and you may feel down. Remember, some job openings receive over 50 proposals from freelancers all over the world, so resilience and tenacity are vital when seeking your first job. After all, there are over 180,000 job postings on this particular freelancer site at any moment of time, and even more on other freelance sites.

It can be difficult to land your first project unless you fit the criteria of what the project is asking from you. Fortunately, I met the criteria for my first job opening. Once you do get your first job, the ball really starts rolling. Some types of jobs are definitely a lot easier to find depending on the supply and demand of such skills in the first place.

Basically, once you have good client reviews and examples of your work to showcase, more people will hire you. I'd also recommend having some sort of official certificate such as an IELTS exam or another specific accreditation on your profile so that the client knows that you're legitimate.

Was your experience in your first freelancing job a positive one?

My first job experience was generally positive. The client was really friendly and concise about what they wanted out of the assignment. They gave me a template to work with and set up a goal describing what the project would be about before sending me the final offer and contract. They were a small publisher who released guides and series of books about the stories and experiences of people's lives in different countries. There were some communication delays due to a four-hour time zone difference between us, thus some messages took a day to be responded to.

Nonetheless, they provided me with good comprehensive feedback and were very attentive to all of my queries too. Not to mention, they paid me quite handsomely. As such, I have maintained a good relationship with the client, and they have also aspired to work with me in the near future on other projects as well. I was glad to have had a great experience with my first client, as not only did it give me a positive impression, but also an understanding of how and who to approach in order to get a good job.

What are your hopes as a freelancer? How far do you see your potential as a freelancer?

My hope for the future is to use my freelancing career as an opportunity to gain a side income during my time studying at university. As well as the money, I would use it as a way to maintain my written English skills, especially because I haven't been able to use my English as often as I wanted to.

I see freelancing as a great way to break out of the monotony of whatever you're doing with your life, whether it's studying or working, because it allows us to do something completely new, and work with new people too. I also see freelancing as a great way for many students to put their knowledge of what they learn in class into practice, (especially those studying computer science, arts and design, statistics or languages).

Freelancing work can also be used to help people to land internships, which are becoming much harder to find and increasingly unpaid. Freelancing on the other hand, guarantees that you'll get paid for your work.

Finally, freelancing platforms are a perfect place to begin establishing a network of employers who may hire you in the long run, as is stated in many job postings. I hope that I'm able to maintain a working relationship with many of my clients so that I continue to work with them on more projects where I can provide meaningful content.

A word of wisdom for others wanting to get into freelancing work online

The best tip that I could give is to be patient. Take the time to make your profile stand out from your competitors, but also know that it can take time to find the right job. After all, you're not the only freelancer on the market. A client may want to work with you because you have specific skills and knowledge that other freelancers don't have. For instance, the client may want freelancers from specific geographical areas or who speak specific languages; these are often defining key criteria for many of the job openings across the different platforms.

So, find out what you're good at and which skills you have that are in high demand at the moment. I was able to work as a writer writing about current affairs in Thailand and Southeast Asia where I'm currently based, and as such, this niche skill worked really well overall.

Another tip is to never push yourself too far. Always start out with jobs that are either entry level or intermediate, unless you're skilled and have experiences through a mainstream career already. If you don't meet the client's expectations, negative reviews for your first few jobs will kill any future opportunities that you have on the online platforms that you use, and you'll have to start all over again from square one.

Additionally, beware of scammers and clients whose payments haven't been verified as there's the off chance that they may not pay you for your work. However, 90% of the time the clients are very friendly and approachable, including the clients whose jobs I'm currently working on.

Finally, the last piece of advice I can give is to take action. You won't get anywhere if you don't take the initiative to make it happen, so get on your computer or tablet and make that freelancing career happen.

Get Your First Job as a Freelancer

Trust yourself and work hard

Ishtiyaq Hussain - Pakistan

Why did you want to become a freelancer? How did you get started?

I am a professional freelance content writer and an undergraduate student. I started my freelance career in November 2020. Since then, I have completed over 20 projects and earned over $1000 from different social media and freelancing platforms. I could have earned more than that but due to my college studies, I couldn't invest much time in freelancing.

Before November 2020, I didn't know anything about freelancing. I was just a simple writer. I loved to write essays and give my opinions on different topics. I didn't know that one could earn from writing content. One day, while talking to a friend, I came to know about freelancing. He told me that there is something called "freelancing" and that I could actually earn through it; I could sell my services as a writer and get paid for them.

I was surprised. I went home and started watching videos online related to freelancing. After watching a lot of videos, I came to know that it's better to start from social media groups instead of signing up to a professional freelancing platform. So, I joined content writing groups on social media and started hunting for jobs. Unfortunately, I couldn't get any jobs. The competition was high and not many people were willing to hire a newbie. However, I kept working hard and made a portfolio on another website where I uploaded all of my writing samples. Next, I made a profile on a popular freelancing website.

How long did it take you to get your first client? Was it hard to get?

Landing your first online freelance job can be a challenging task. In my opinion, this is one of the most difficult phases in a freelancer's journey. Personally, this was the most difficult time for me.

I thought that once I learned a skill, it would be easier to land a job. But it turned out that the opposite was true.

However, I didn't lose any hope and continued applying for jobs on the online freelancing site through buyer requests. After bidding for 25 days straight on 190 job posts, I landed my first ever freelance job. The job was to research 20 case studies and rewrite them. Although it was a difficult job and the pay rate was very low, I still decided to do it. The client was happy with my work and left me 5 stars and an excellent rating. I was happy that all of my hard work had paid off.

Once I received a rating on my profile, the journey became much easier. More clients started replying to my job proposals. In less than 7 days after completing my first job, I got my second job. The second job continued for a whole month. I wrote 9 video scripts for my client and earned my first 100 dollars.

Was your experience in your first freelancing job a positive one?

In the first-ever freelance job that I completed, the experience was both a good and a bad one. I had mixed feelings regarding that job. I was new to the freelance market and didn't know how to negotiate prices and deadlines.

Even though the pay rate was very low. I accepted the job because I had been struggling to secure my first job. The project was harder than I thought and took me 8 days to complete the job. Whilst I was happy that I now had a rating on my profile and had earned my first dollar, a part of me was unhappy.

That's when I learned my first lesson - never work at pay rates that are too low. You should know the worth of the hard work that you're putting in.

The second lesson I learned after completing my first job was that you need to learn other important skills, like good communication and negotiation skills, to survive in the freelance market. You can be amazing at what you do, but if you can't communicate well, you'll most likely miss the opportunity. Clients should be quite easy to come across if you're generally good at negotiating and communication.

What are your hopes as a freelancer? How far do you see your potential as a freelancer?

Freelancing is becoming more and more popular around the world. It has a bright future ahead of it, and its demand is increasing globally. Over the last decade, the freelance economy has risen at an exponential rate. According to an American study, approximately 60% of the world's workers will be freelancers by 2027. I think that freelancing is an amazing career choice if you are passionate about your skills and want to get paid for them. It allows you to work with amazing clients and there is a lot of room for self-improvement.

For me, it has been an amazing freelance journey to this day. Even though some days were full of stress, where I couldn't land any job, I'm still happy with what I have accomplished so far. Freelancing has helped me both individually and economically. I have both learned a lot and earned more than my expectations for the time frame. My writing skills and communication skills have improved. These skills have helped me in my professional life as well as when freelancing.

I feel that with the way the freelancing industry is rising, one could certainly consider a career in it. Personally, I am completely satisfied with what I'm doing. I enjoy freelance writing. It allows me to meet new people around the world and learn from them. There is huge potential in it and I would love to have a career in it.

A word of wisdom for others wanting to get into freelancing work online

If you want to work as a freelancer, you should know that it requires a lot of hard work and patience. There will be times when you won't have a job for many days and you will think about quitting the field. In these difficult times, you need to be patient, trust yourself and work hard. If you are planning to start your career as a freelancer, keep the following 4 things in mind. Remember, these are my personal opinions from what I have experienced so far in this journey:

Go niche: "Don't be a jack of all trades". When I was looking for general projects like article writing, they received 50+ proposals in two minutes. I concluded that there should be another way to get a reply, other than being the fastest to submit the proposal. So, I looked for a service in which I could use the same skills, but there won't be so much competition. I came up with these niches: Amazon product descriptions, non-fiction e-books, and SEO content writing. Try to find not-so-obvious places where your skills can be used. And of course, learn new skills which have a higher demand and lower competition.

Upgrade your skills. Stay up to date with market trends and secure your freelancing career's future.

Set realistic expectations. When it comes to time and money, be realistic. If your client's deadline is unrealistic, be open and honest about what you can accomplish within the period. Some clients expect you to do anything they want, while the finest clients pay attention and adapt to your needs. Watch out for these good clients and build long-term relationships with them.

Try, try and try: There are numerous ups and downs as a freelancer. Some days will be difficult, but you must learn from them. The road to becoming a successful freelancer is not without its difficulties!

Get Your First Job as a Freelancer

Stay calm, don't think you are not going to make it

Diego Navarro - El Salvador

Why did you want to become a freelancer? How did you get started?

Well, I started because I needed some money. I live in a 3rd world country, so finding a good job with good pay is almost impossible. It was at the point that freelancing was better than an actual traditional job here, so a friend of mine showed me an online freelancing platform that he had been working on. He told me that with hard work and a little bit of luck, I could start making a good amount of money as a freelancer. That's what I was after - a job that pays well.

Besides that, the fact that I could work in my own time was just perfect for me. I was already working as a freelancer in my country, so I knew how to deal with different clients. I also liked the challenge to work of working with people who didn't know me and giving them a good impression.

How long did it take you to get your first client? Was it hard to get?

I was a little bit lucky, because I got my first client within the first week of creating my profile. I read that a lot of people had faced the problem of not being able to get any jobs for months because nobody trusted them. I was afraid that this would happen to me, but fortunately I was hired quickly.

My first job was kind of hard to get, but because I sent a lot of proposals, each application was better than the last one. I had more opportunities to impress the potential clients and then one day, out of nowhere, I had my first interview. I was super excited that I could finally start working as an online freelancer.

The hardest part for me was the wait, because you don't know if you are ever going to find your first job. Everyone wants the best prospects for their jobs, right? So, I thought about the possibility that I would never get a job.

Since my native language is Spanish, all of my experience had been in Spanish up to that point, so it was pretty much impossible for me to showcase my experience on the freelancing platform, because I needed some experience writing in English. Luckily, I got my first chance, and I try to do my best in each of the jobs that I get.

Was your experience in your first freelancing job a positive one?

It was positive. The client was very polite, and I had a lot of respect for him because he gave me the chance to start up on the platform. The work was hard, but it wasn't anything that I hadn't done before so I knew I was up for the task. We only communicated maybe once a day when I delivered the parts of the job that he wanted done, and also when he would share suggestions that could make my work better.

Overall, my first client is a very special person to me. Because of him, I've now had more work. He gave me the first opportunity to prove myself and to show people that I can do a great job. Hopefully more people have the luck that I did so they can also prove themselves and excel.

What are your hopes as a freelancer? How far do you see your potential as a freelancer?

I hope to make a living out of online freelancing, I really do, because right now it's such a perfect job for me. I work in what I like, the hours and days that I want, and I set my own rate. The thing that I love the most is working from home. Whilst hopes are very high, but I know it's not going to be easy to make consistent income every month. I'm just starting off, so I have to make a name as an online freelancer.

Maybe in the future I'll get a long-term contract. I think that's my short term goal - to get a long-term job, know that I will have consistent income and get food to my table every day, and that I can enjoy life. So, if I work hard, and grind my way to a long-term job, I think that both my expectations and my potential as an online freelancer will increase more.

A word of wisdom for others wanting to get into freelancing work online

Stay calm, don't think you are not going to make it. The worst thing that happened to me was thinking that I was never going to get a job, or that I may only get one or two. Whenever you get your first job, don't think about the amount of money you are going to get. Think about the quality of work you want to provide. This will ensure that the client will be impressed with your job and leave a very good review. Reviews are everything when you are just starting.

It doesn't matter if it is 5 or 100 dollars, what matters is to build a good reputation with your name and get more experience with every work you complete. Keep going until you get the big job you always wanted and you're earning what you know you deserve. Then, people will know your worth and they won't let you go. Going above and beyond what they ask of you on the project is going to help you lots.

Afterword

A friend once asked me "Arthur, do you think our generation has it tough? Or has it been like this for every generation?"

As I read the stories, a common theme did sneak through, where people had to adjust quickly to the current pandemic. It may be tough to get work and there may be a lot of competition, but are we really worse off than what our parents or grandparents went through?

So, I wanted to close off by telling you a bit more about what happened with the pivot I made at the start of this book - approaching the niche market and standing out from the crowd.

It took me a while to get the first client, and we were so happy when we did. I found out how and why they chose us, and we looked after the client well. From there, I made sure that I strengthened certain areas of our business processes to gain more of the same type of clients. Hard work followed, writing letters to potential referrers, writing more articles for my website, and more late nights.

2 to 3 years later, I had 2 staff dedicated to this new market and we had a 2 month waiting list for our services. I had no more space to fit any more staff in the allocated area, my website had articles covering most of the first page in search engines, and I had begun to think further about how to niche in this niched area!

Many years have passed now, and even up to today, the 2 staff that I had are still running their own businesses in this market.

So, I encourage you, if you are a freelancer, to give it your best. We don't know what is around the corner. We can't predict the future. However, I know that if you fight and succeed, you will find out how successful you can become, and how far that success can travel.

Get Your First Job as a Freelancer

Get Your First Job as a Freelancer

If you enjoyed this book you can visit our website to read many more stories.

arthurlee.com.au

More Titles to come!

www.ingramcontent.com/pod-product-compliance
Lightning Source LLC
Chambersburg PA
CBHW052338220526
45472CB00001B/481